SWEET NUTCRACKER

David Rossoff

This book is for my sons Paul and Simon, and my beloved grandson, Jamie.

By the same author
BIBLE STORIES RETOLD
THE BOOK OF WITNESSES
THE THREE DONKEYS
THE VOICES OF MASADA
THE LITTLE BOOK OF SYLVANUS
'YOU HAVE A MINUTE, LORD?'
A SMALL TOWN IS A WORLD

SWEET NUTCRACKER

by

David Kossoff

illustrated by

IONICUS

ROBSON BOOKS

The illustrations to Sweet Nutcracker *are dedicated to*
Tafool Amer Salim Al Mashini of Oman.

FIRST PUBLISHED IN GREAT BRITAIN IN 1985 BY ROBSON BOOKS
LTD., BOLSOVER HOUSE, 5-6 CLIPSTONE STREET, LONDON W1P 7EB.
COPYRIGHT © 1985 DAVID KOSSOFF.

British Library Cataloguing in Publication Data

   Kossoff, David
     Sweet nutcracker
     I. Title
   823′.914 (F)   PR6061.08

   ISBN 0-86051-329-7

Printed in Hungary

INTRODUCTION

This story is based upon one of 'The Tales of Hoffman' and a word or two about Hoffman would seem in place here, for he was in his own way as remarkable as one of the many characters in his tales.

He was very clever indeed. He was an artist, composer and author. He was short, wiry, good-looking and a brilliant talker, his words full of wit and fantasy. He had a puckish face with dark lively eyes. He was full of movement, his hands and body never still, like a puppet on strings.

He wrote marvellously about music, using the pen-name Kreisler. He was the most widely-read and popular critic of his time. He had unerring taste for the best and the new. He was one of the first to write of J. S. Bach and of Beethoven (who was very grateful). He drew attention to Weber, and to Schumann (who called one of his piano pieces Kreisleriana).

Ernst Theodor Wilhelm Hoffmann was born in 1776, in Königsburg, East Prussia. He was of a legal family, and attended the Königsberg University, where soon he was giving as much time to the Arts as to law and philosophy. He was a diligent pupil, working hard at everything. He graduated at 19 with high honours.

He was a brilliant young man. Gifted, versatile and well liked. He was also indiscreet and impatient with any sort of authority. He was in trouble with such authority many times. He was part of that same 'authority'. He was a civil servant, with always excellent marks in the promotion examinations, but his inclination to satirize, to poke fun, in caricature and words, interfered with his advancement and he would find himself serving in remote small towns instead of the cities he loved. There were a number of such exiles in his life, but he turned them always to good account. He would devote all his spare time to his music and painting — and his great skill with words. He became widely known and respected as a writer. By the time he was 30, with the help of an influential friend called Hippel (who was to get him out of trouble many times later) he was in Warsaw. There he founded and conducted an orchestra, soon playing his own works. His civil service superiors were happier with him and all seemed secure.

Napoleon spoiled it. In 1806 Prussia had fallen to the French and soon Warsaw was taken. Hoffmann, a civil servant, was out of a job. Life became hard. He supported his wife and child as best he could, as a musician and scene-painter. A year later, refusing to take an oath of allegiance to the French, he was deported, alone, to Berlin, where he nearly starved. Soon, dreadful news from home: his infant daughter had died. His wife was allowed to join him and he took any work he could find.

Things improved. He was given the post of Theatre Director in Bamberg in South Germany, a place of lively culture. He was tireless. In the next five years he produced and directed every kind of play, often writing the incidental music also. Away from the theatre he wrote opera and many instrumental works. He translated from the French and wrote articles for many musical magazines (as 'Kreisler'). It is said that much of his writing was done on the tables of Bamberg inns, for he loved good company and good wine.

There was a darker side to him. His health was not robust and the death of his daughter brought periods of deep depression, of illness and exhaustion. He was brave, even foolhardy. In the later Napoleonic Wars he was often at the front with a troupe of actors and singers, entertaining the troops. He seemed fearless and was once wounded. He wrote of these times and battles — and sold the book manuscript for a cellar of wine!

From 1814 his life was smoother. He returned to public service and became a judge in the Supreme Court, very conscientious and just. He composed less and wrote more. Criticism, articles and novels, and stories, the 'Tales', which were soon famous and eagerly awaited.

But he had not quite lost his weakness for satire, and in 1820 was again in trouble with his superiors, but they were lenient, for he was ill. Overwork and heavy drinking had taken their toll. He had digestive and liver complaints. His nervous system was affected. He became progressively paralysed. He died in 1822, very poor. He was 46.

The tales of Hoffmann are far better known than his music. Many composers used his stories, notably Offenbach in his *Tales of Hoffmann* and Delibes, for his *Coppelia* ballet. Although Hoffmann was not himself a 'great' composer, he had original musical ideas which influenced later, larger talents.

He himself was much influenced by Mozart — so much so that he changed his middle name from Wilhelm to Amadeus!

'The Tale of the Nutcracker and the Mouse King' was written in 1816 as part of a Christmas collection of stories for children. It attracted Alexander Dumas the elder, who translated and adapted it and worked with Tchaikovsky to create the full-length ballet. The 'story within the story', not used in the ballet, of Princess Pirlipatine and the Krakatuk Nut, is the story used as the basis for *Sweet Nutcracker*.

D.K., 1985

YOU never knew quite where you were with Doctor Drosselmeyer. Even his title, Doctor, was a bit misleading, for he wasn't just a pills and medicine Doctor at all. Not at all. Mind you, he did put things right. Often more right than they were before. He seemed able to mend anything. To make anything, in fact. If you were one of his many godchildren (for he had no children of his own and nobody had ever heard of a *Mrs* Drosselmeyer) and he gave you one of his marvellous toys or puppets you were never quite sure what you were getting. You never quite knew with the Doctor. As he gave it to you he would look at you with his one very bright eye that seemed to know what you were thinking and he would say, "Love it and respect it and it will never go wrong. For love and respect make anything work."

You never knew what you were getting. Toy soldiers would march and shout commands and write letters home and when they'd done their time retire on half pay. Clockwork birds would fly out of the nursery window to visit friends and lay eggs and take baths in the fountain. You just never knew.

China dolls in silken crinolines would whisper behind their fans as you walked past, and other dolls would *not* make remarks, and take your hand, and you could tell them secret things and they'd never breathe a word. If you looked in the window of a doll's house made by the Doctor you might see a party going on, or a Grand Ball, or a concert. Once, it was said, in such a house, there was a fire, and the toy firemen and engine from next door rushed in and dealt with it.

The Doctor was of strange appearance. Only one eye, as I said. Over the other, a black eye-patch. He was very pale and very tall and thin. He was very stooped, with long arms and hands, which had long bony fingers. His nose and chin were long also and he was completely bald. To cover the baldness he wore a wig made of glass which he'd made himself. Unlike the wigs worn by most people at that time it was always clean and no insects lived in it. Sometimes on the wig he wore a skull-cap of velvet with a long tassel.

He always looked the same. He wore a very shabby braided frock coat of faded yellow brocade, a long waistcoat of the same material, with many pockets, black silk breeches and knee-high boots. He did not change his clothes for anybody. Nobody knew if he was rich or poor. Nobody had ever been invited to his house. He spoke in the same way to everyone. He liked children very much indeed but was very choosy with grown-ups. He was very widely known and in those houses he would agree to visit he was always welcome.

You might ask how did the Doctor come to be so bent over and shabby and bald and one-eyed? Well, there is a story, and it has all the answers — and everything else a good story should have. I tell you this and you can trust my opinion, for I also like children, of any age, and I would not tell you wrong.

Once upon a time (for it is that kind of story) far away in another land there was a small Kingdom, and in the towns and villages there was great happiness and excitement for the exquisitely beautiful Princess Pirlipatine was soon to be one year old. The flags and bunting were going up, the bands and choirs were practising, the soldiers were polishing everything in sight and drilling and stamping and shouting without pause.

At the Palace the excitement was even greater, for the baby was a great favourite with everybody. Not only was she the long-awaited only child of the King and Queen, she was as beautiful inside as out. Everybody loved her and she deserved it. She had been born with perfect teeth and her beautiful smile enchanted everybody. The Queen lived in a sort of quiet glow of happiness. She was rather a quiet sort of person. The King was not. He had a loud voice and liked to give orders. He would get an idea and stick to it even when (sometimes) his idea wasn't very good. He would gather the whole palace staff in the Great Ballroom and tell them the idea and give them his orders.

Which is what he was doing this morning.

"No more mice!" he told them in his orders voice. "The Princess is to grow up in a palace free of mice. No more mice. Mice steal, and spoil things, and are unhealthy and make noises in the night. They frighten the chambermaids and the undercooks and it's gone on too long. I have sent a message to my old friend the good Doctor Drosselmeyer who is god-father to the Princess and he will tell us how to get rid of the mice. He arrives today and everybody will do as he says. That's all. Back to work."

Later that day the Doctor arrived with a roll of his fine drawings under his arm. He called a meeting right away of the Palace carpenters, springmakers, wire-benders and those who knew where the tools were left last time. The King also came. The Doctor pinned up the drawings.

"Number one," he said, "shows a flat piece of wood with a pulled-back strong spring fixed to it at one end. At the other end a spring release with a small spike for a piece of cheese or fat or bread. The mouse comes, goes to eat, releases the spring which comes over — whack. End of mouse. Observe the working model. Thus and thus, whack. End of mouse."

The craftsmen and the King were amazed.

"Amazing!" said the King. "What do you call this remarkable invention?"

"A mousetrap," said the Doctor. And started to give detailed orders for the making of hundreds. The King wanted to add an order or two also but the Doctor looked at him with his piercing eye and the King kept quiet.

Mind you, there were plenty of other orders for him to give. There never was such an excitement at the Palace, both upstairs and downstairs, inside and out.

The Doctor's mousetraps were a great success, and the King was mightily pleased and was giving thought to creating some special sort of honour for the Doctor, who didn't care about such things much one way or the other. He stayed in the Palace, mending every clock and musical box and door lock and cooking spit in sight. Every now and then he would sit with the Queen who seemed, as the hundreds of mice were taken away for disposal, not as happy as you might think. One day she confided in the Doctor.

"All the mice were of the same clan," he told him. "A vast family, going back many generations. They have been in the Palace far longer than the King's family and in some ways I suppose had at least as much right here as we have."

The Doctor entirely disagreed (he had no use at all for mice) but kept silent, for he had respect for the gentle Queen.

"The present Head of the clan," she said, "the Mouse Queen if you like, whom I've known since I was a girl, is Dame Rodentia."

"*Is?*" said the Doctor, who was rather proud of his invention.

"She is far too clever," said the Queen gently, "to be tempted by one of your little traps. She is old, and worthy of respect. But she is vengeful and has in the past taken revenge for something that upset her. We changed our cheese supplier once and she sent out a call to all the mice in the land to block up the pipes. A national stoppage. We changed back. I promised her. We understand each other. She will not forgive this of the wiping out of the clan. Of that I am sure. I know her. And, neither will her son, who, it is said, is a fearsome fighter with seven heads."

"Seven heads?" said the Doctor, who had scientific interest in such things.

"Each one with a golden crown, for he will be King Mouse upon his mother's death," said the Queen.

"Try not to worry," said the Doctor. "I will evolve a twenty-four-hour protection for my godchild. Leave it to me."

The Queen cheered up for there was much to do and the last few days before the Birthday were hectic. Then the Day came. A perfect day for a perfect Baby. The Palace shone with welcome. From far and wide came the guests, and when they were gathered in the Great Ballroom the anticipation was immense!

Then it was time, and at the far end the huge doors opened and the great crowd drew back, leaving the centre clear for what was to come. It was a sight to see! First the state trumpeters, to their positions. Then came children, scattering rose petals. Now the fanfare — and in danced the *corps de ballet* of the state opera. Then the ministers of the crown and their ladies. Oh, the colour and the pomp! Then the King and Queen. And *then*, on a platform carried by ten splendid footmen, the Princess Pirlipatine, in a solid gold highchair! It was the Procession of the Baby!

Far away from the Ballroom, down in the wine cellar, over in the farthest corner, there was not any celebration going on at all. In the darkness glittered eight pairs of eyes. One pair belonged to the Mouse Queen, Rodentia, and the other seven to her son, who was holding his violent temper in check and keeping his seven mouths shut, for his Mother was speaking and you do not interrupt when Mother is speaking.

"We are the only ones left," said the Queen. "The whole clan has been wiped out by that Doctor pig.

Well, my son, it is not the end of the matter. I will take my revenge! Not upon the Doctor pig or the King or Queen, but upon the Baby!"

Her son exchanged glances with one or two of his heads, then spoke, in his usual way.

"Not a chance, old darlin'! Pipe dreams! Old lady's fancies. Give it up, me old mum. Forget it. The Doctor pig has mounted a twenty-four-hour guard. In the nursery at night six nurses sit around the cot. Each one with a large cat on her lap! Each one strokes, each one purrs. A disgustin' noise — and a very discouragin' sight. Forget it, me old squeaker. Not a chance!"

"I have been observing the ring of nurses," said the Mouse Queen, "and have learned much. They do not speak to each other for fear of disturbing the Baby.

They stroke the cats and the cats purr, which makes the strokers sleepy. They fall asleep and the stroking stops and the cats fall asleep too."

"What, *all* of 'em?" said her son, with his seven sets of whiskers twitching.

"Not *yet*," said his mother. "Not yet, but the night will come when all of them *do*. And I will visit the beautiful Princess in her cot and with one small bite I will cast a spell that will make them all wish they'd never *seen* a mousetrap!" She looked deep into her son's fourteen eyes. "Every night you will keep watch, each head in turn. And rest assured, the night will come. You will wake me, and you and your Mother will use routes only they know to the cot, and the thing will be done."

And the night did come, and off they went along dark secret ways to do the dreadful thing.

In the nursery it was very quiet, except for the soft snoring of the eldest nurse and the sleepy spluttering of the nightlight candles. The Mouse Queen had vanished as silently as she had appeared.

Suddenly one of the cats woke. A powerful hunter of a cat called Murr. There was a smell of mouse! He leapt high, with a curse, and so did his stroker, as his claws sank into her lap! In a moment, everyone was awake, rushing about and accusing each other of falling asleep on duty.

Then the youngest nurse thought to look in the cot — and fainted dead away!

The golden-haired blue-eyed dimpled smiling beautiful Pirlipatine was now an ugly pinched-faced creature with ratty mouse-coloured hair — and *spots*!

Pandemonium! When the Queen saw her baby she also fainted dead away, into the King's arms. The poor King, no less heartbroken, started to shout about baby-switching and kidnap — and to give lots of orders, many contradicting each other. Suddenly Doctor Drosselmeyer was in the room, observing everything, even the tiny bite on the baby's left ear lobe. He helped revive the Queen and they both knew that it was the work of the Mouse Queen. It was the dreaded revenge.

The Doctor spoke to the King, sharply. "Lower your voice a moment and listen to me. This is no kidnap or substitution. This is poor Perlipatine, changed by a wicked spell. Perlipatine, my little god-daughter. I am going to shut myself away with your Court Astrologer, who is an old friend, and we will not sleep or rest until we have found a way to break the spell. Trust me. In the meantime," said the the Doctor, who knew the King would need something to do, "give orders. Send emissaries and messengers to every part of your Kingdom. Offer rewards to anyone who can help."

Privately the Doctor did not think it would do much good, but he was old and wise. Wise enough to know that you never can tell.

"Right!" said the King, and gathered the staff in Ballroom. "Right!" he said to them all. "Emissaries and messengers to go off in all directions! Right away! In all directions! Off you go!" And off they went!

At the Palace the Queen wept and the King waited for news and everybody walked softly and nobody smiled at all. Once or twice the Doctor was seen looking down at the poor Princess, deep in thought, then he would disappear again. At the end of the fourth day he went to the King and Queen.

"We have it," he said. "We wasted two days following wrong tracks but then I noticed two important things that have not changed in the Princess. The perfect teeth she was born with and her liking for nuts. We then changed our line of scientific and astrological research and we have it. It is the Krakatuk Nut!"

"The what?" said the King.

"The Krakatuk Nut," said the Doctor. "The Princess must eat the kernel of the Krakatuk Nut. The hardest nut known to man. Very rare indeed. The Nut must be cracked by a young man using his teeth. It must be a young man who has never shaved, has always worn boots, and can walk backwards with his eyes closed without stumbling."

"This is absolutely wonderful!" said the King. "Wonderful! We'll do it tomorrow morning first thing when the Princess wakes up — and the young man can stay to lunch. Wonderful."

The Doctor felt sad, for the Queen's smile had begun to come back.

"We have neither the Nut nor the young man," he said. "None of the books or stars tell where the Nut may be found, and such young men are also very rare. We leave immediately, armed with a complete set of signs and portents, and we will go wherever they lead us."

"How long?" said the King and Queen together.

"Who can say?" said the Doctor. "Who can say? Here, for the Princess, two presents. A little man of wood with a hinged cape that makes him a nutcracker. Let her love the Nutcracker. If she loses him, as she may, she will find him again. The little sword she will not lose."

"Presents?" said the Queen sadly. "How long, Doctor?"

Again the Doctor said "Who can say?" and left them.

Little did he know that the search would take nearly fifteen years. It would take him and the poor Astrologer right round the world, to freezing cold places and to hot damp jungles full of noises at night and crawly things. They would search deep valleys and visit wise men at the tops of mountains. They would know thirst and hunger and great poverty.

Savage tribes would attack them and the Doctor would lose an eye. All their luggage would be stolen and they would have to wear (and sleep in) the same clothes for years. The Doctor would go absolutely bald with worry of it all. Nearly fifteen years, and most of the time in far-off lonely remote *mysterious* places.

 are now back at the Palace. The poor Princess is now sixteen years old and, although a pleasant enough person, very plain indeed, with a pale spotty skin and a slight cast in one eye.

Her nose is thin and bony and her forehead too high. She is lumpy-looking and rather clumsy. She is fat where she should be slim and thin where she should be fat. And none of the Court hairdressers can do a thing with that mousy hair. Her only good feature is the perfect teeth she shows when she smiles — which is not often.

The King and Queen are older and greyer. The Palace is a sad place, for a spell put on one member of a family affects all the others.

It is Wednesday. Tea-time. The butler comes to tell the King that two men are asking to see him.

"Why didn't you let them in?" asked the King. "I like visitors, and nobody comes any more."

The butler was embarrassed. "They look like tramps, Your Majesty," he said. "They are dressed in rags. One is short and the other is tall and thin and bent and bald with a black eye-patch."

"Doesn't sound like anybody *I* know," said the King. "Friends of yours, my dear?" he asked the Queen.

The Queen had a funny feeling suddenly. "Did they *say* anything?" she said.

"Something about a nut," said the butler.

"Show 'em in!" shouted the King. It was the Astrologer and the Doctor and they had found the Nut! Oh, the welcome they were given! The huggings and handshakings and the long hot baths — with the King's own bathrobes to wrap themselves in till their new clothes were ready. And then the huge supper that went on till nearly midnight ending with sweets and nuts and wine. There was so much to tell. Of the endless searchings and journeys, the adventures, the funny bits, the bad times. The King and Queen told their news too. Not a sign of a mouse, said the Queen, since that awful night so long ago.

The Princess, allowed to stay up, said little. She was rather shy of this strange-looking man with one eye who it seemed was her godfather. Often she felt that one eye looking across the table at her. Then the Doctor said to her, "Would you like to crack a nut for me with the Nutcracker doll I once gave you?"

The Princess blushed. "I don't know where it is," she said, "I've lost it."

The Doctor seemed in no way upset.

"Were you sad to lose him?" he asked.

"Yes, I was," said the Princess. "I loved him," — and then blushed again.

"Then you will find him again," said the Doctor. "Positively."

"Did you find the young man too?" asked the King. "Or shall we make it into a nationwide contest that any young man with powerful jaws and teeth can enter, with a very big money prize to the winner."

The Doctor paused. He *had* found the young man, but had a bigger plan for him than a very big money prize. A plan that had love in it, for the Princess too.

"Good idea," said the Doctor to the King. And in no time there were selectors and county heats and seedings and early rounds and eliminators and expert commentators and quarter finals all over the country, using harder and harder nuts. There were many finalists. Hundreds, for the money prize was huge. Then came the day and the Men's Finals were held in the Centre Court. The Palace. The finalists were confident, in top condition, dauntless.

But this was the Krakatuk Nut. Teeth splintered by the thousand, jaws were dislocated, neck muslces twanged like bowstrings, sweat poured, eyes started from the head in the hopeless strain of it all. The Nut showed no mark at all. Everybody went home. Great gloom at the Palace.

"What were those *other* things?" said the King to the Doctor. "Something about boots?"

"A young man," said the Doctor, "who has never shaved, has always worn boots, and can walk backwards with his eyes closed without stumbling."

"Well," said the King, a bit discouraged, "let's try again. A new contest. A bigger prize."

"Let us," said the Doctor, more to the Queen than the King, "make the prize the hand of the Princess in marriage. She is old enough to marry, and deserves happiness."

It was agreed, and announced. There were twenty-six entrants. And the result was exactly the same. As the teeth were being swept up the Doctor took the King to one side.

"A late entry," he said. "Number 27. I have great confidence in him and will sponsor him myself. He has all the qualifications needed. He has never shaved, has been a brilliant horseman since a child and never out of riding boots, and has both perfect backward-walking co-ordination and the jaw muscles of a lion. He is also, by the way, of great good looks, and most pleasant disposition. I will present him to the Court at midday tomorrow."

And he did. And because the Doctor had a certain style he did it splendidly, in the form of a small procession. First came musicians, then high-stepping dancers dressed as soldiers with glittering boots, then more musicians, and then Number 27, in riding clothes, which make even ugly men look good. And Number 27 was *far* from ugly. Oh, it was a splendid sight!

There sat the Krakatuk Nut, the size of a large walnut but smoother. It sat in a little dish on a high table. Next to it the little silver sword. By the table stood Number 27, whose name was Paul. He knew exactly what he had to do and what the prize was. Opposite to him stood the prize, the Princess. Now he'd had a good look at her, Paul was not sure he wanted to go ahead. For her part, the Princess had no doubts at all. She'd loved him at sight. Paul looked across at the Doctor, whose one brilliant eye seemed to know exactly what he was thinking. The Doctor gave a nod and Paul, who was an honourable person who'd made a promise, picked up the nut and put it between his strong white teeth. The Doctor's eye bored into the nut which had so nearly killed him. There was a silence and then . . . a loud *crackatuk*! Nobody moved. Paul broke the shell

open and with the little silver sword delicately picked out the kernel and gave it to the Princess, who put it in her mouth and ate it. Everyone held their breath. And then before their very eyes the plain spotty mousy shy girl changed into the gorgeous beauty that the blue-eyed golden-haired dimpled baby of long before would have become.

The radiant Pirlipatine, less shy now, smiled at Paul, showing clearly what she felt for him. In a moment he felt the same. Now it was time for the other and simpler part. He closed his eyes and started to walk backwards. Upright, in a perfectly straight line.

Suddenly, from nowhere, the Mouse Queen was under his feet, screeching with anger and hate! He stumbled! His foot came down on her, killing her instantly, and he *fell* heavily. Almost before he hit the floor he began to change. He shrank and became no higher than a hand. Then he became utterly still and turned to wood. He became the lost Nutcracker doll.

The Princess was transfixed. Shocked beyond
belief. She had found her handsome Prince and lost
him again, in seconds. She looked around wildly, her
eyes full of tears. Then she saw her long-lost beloved
Nutcracker doll and lifted it with both hands
lovingly to her cheek. It felt warm and comforting.

Suddenly, again from nowhere, the Mouse Queen's
seven-headed son! With a murderous-looking axe
which he waved in every direction, his seven mouths
cursing and screaming. A frightening horrible noise.
All his eyes glared up at Pirlipatine.

"Your Nutcracker killed my mum!" roared the mouths. They were ugly, wide open, red. "And I will

kill *you*! I'll make you ugly again! And I'll chop up and eat all the things you love best. Startin' with that Nutcracker pig!" The mouths went on shouting and the Princess, terrified, held the Nutcracker tighter to her cheek and kissed him. Then he spoke, very softly, into her ear.

"Give me the little sword," he said. "Put it in my right hand and put me down on the floor. Don't be afraid. We are swordsmen as well as horsemen in our family. Do as I say. Now."

It was a long and terrible fight. The Mouse King was vicious and fought dirty, able to look seven ways at once. But the Nutcracker was brave and fast on his feet and the heads came off one by one. At last it was over and the Nutcracker looked up at the beautiful Pirlipatine and grew again into the handsome Paul, with a bruised head and a slightly wounded arm where the axe had caught him. They fell into each other's arms.

What a wonderful time followed! The Palace came back to life.

The young lovers charmed everyone. They spent every possible minute together, each day loving and respecting each other more. It was noticed that the Princess was never without her new bracelet, of seven small gold crowns. There was to be an engagement party and Paul, who was musical, decided to teach Pirlipatine the betrothal dance of his own country, for them to perform together at the party. He taught the music to the flautists and other

Court musicians. It was a great success. First they danced alone, with great grace, then the court joined in, then again they danced alone, seeing only each other.

After

the engagement party the preparations for the wedding went ahead with great energy. The King and Queen were filled with joy. It was to be the biggest happiest wedding *ever* for this was no ordinary young man with strong teeth and riding boots. No indeed. This was Crown Prince Paul of Confectiana, the Land of Sweets, far away, where

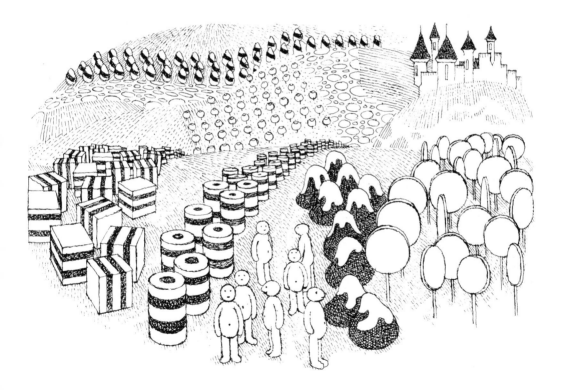

marzipan is mined and sugar-plums and lollipops are grown from seed. Where liquorice is made — of all sorts. Where jelly babies go to kindergarten and wine gums mature in barrels. Where the nuts are *safe* — and have chocolate instead of shells! No one is sure where the Land of Sweets is, and perhaps it is better so.

The invitations went out to every kind of person,

from the grandest to the most humble. The presents started to arrive and were laid out in the smaller Ballroom for people to see.

The Doctor examined them with interest. If any of
them had been damaged in the post he would make it
perfect again. The King and Queen wondered what
the Doctor's own present would be. His gifts to his
godchildren were famous. What, they thought,
would he give to grown-up children?

The Doctor smiled a little to himself and seemed to become a gardener, choosing a slope opposite the

wing of the Palace where the newly-weds were to have their bedchamber. He worked alone, surrounded by seedlings and pots and his large box of tools and instruments. He did not welcome visitors.

At the Wedding, which was quite beyond description so I won't try, the Doctor seemed like a thin bent benevolent spirit. He spoke and ate little, watching the beautiful Pirlipatine and her handsome husband spread their own happiness round them like warmth.

Late in the evening he took them aside a moment. "After the last guest has gone," he said, "and the Palace at last is quiet and you have prepared for bed, go out on to your balcony and look across at the sloping garden. There will be a full moon. Do not speak. There will be a silence. No birds will sing. You will hear music. Then a star will fall, and dance

among the flowers, to wake them. Then they will dance. For you. A waltz. It is my present to you, my young lovers. The Waltz of the Flowers."